Museums in the World

Top 40 Must-See Museums Around the World

Melissa Hammock

I0480562

DEDICATION

Contents

10 Tips to Make a Museum Visit More Interesting

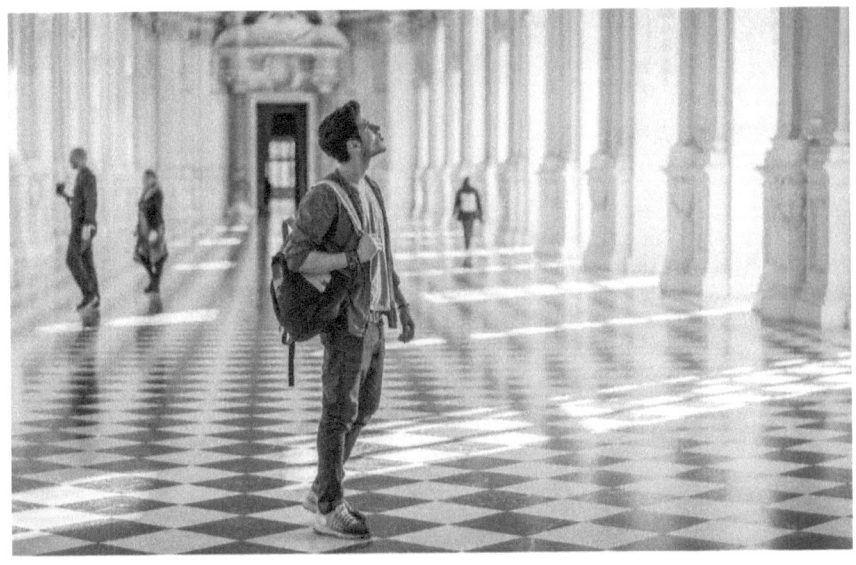

Museums are among the most popular attractions in the famous cities of the world, but they can also be boring. Ask many travellers to be honest and they'll often say that they go to museums out of obligation, not out of interest. But museums are also unparalleled in terms of historical interest and detail. If you want to learn about the past, you can't afford to skip museums. So if you do want to see treasures of the past, but are worried about being bored, how can you make a museum tour more interesting? We have a few ideas. The following are 10 tips to make a museum visit more interesting. These ideas have as much to do with how you approach a museum visit as the visit itself, but they should help you make the most of a trip to one of the world's great museums, whether in France, Italy, England, or China.

Don't feel obligated to go to a museum

This is an easy first step. Don't go to the museum in the first place if you don't like museums. Sure, it can feel weird to skip the Louvre in Paris or the British Museum in London, but if you know that deep down, you'll be bored to death or have no interest in history, why spend the time doing something you hate? Vacations should be tailored around your interests and if you have no interest in museums, no amount of finessing the experience will make you suddenly like it.

That being said, don't automatically discount a museum if you think that your modern attention span cannot handle it. Travel is a great way to slow down the pace of your ordinary life and have new experiences, and a trip to a museum can be that experience for a lot of travellers.

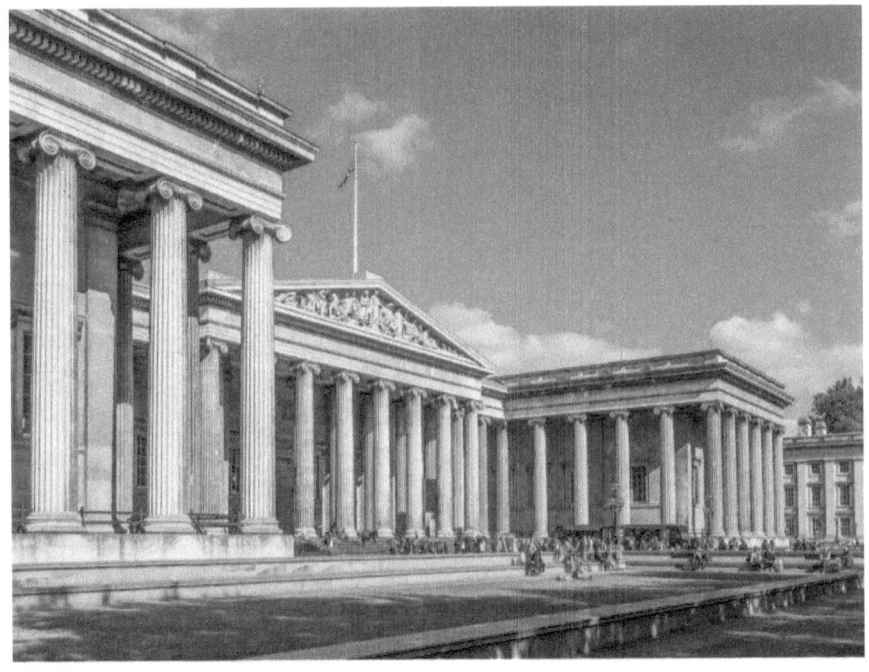

British Museum in London, England

Check wait times before you go

This one is key. Some museums are very popular and you'll have a lot better time in the museum if you don't have to wait 45 minutes before you get in. At the Vatican Museums in Rome, for instance, you can book a "skip the line" ticket that gets you around the potentially hours-long wait to get into St. Peter's Basilica and the Museums. For other museums that are known to have lineups to get in, simply check the website ahead of time to see what the estimated wait time is. Going at off-peak times like lunchtime and near the end of the day will often mean fewer visitors, so if you don't plan on staying long at the museum, this is a good option too.

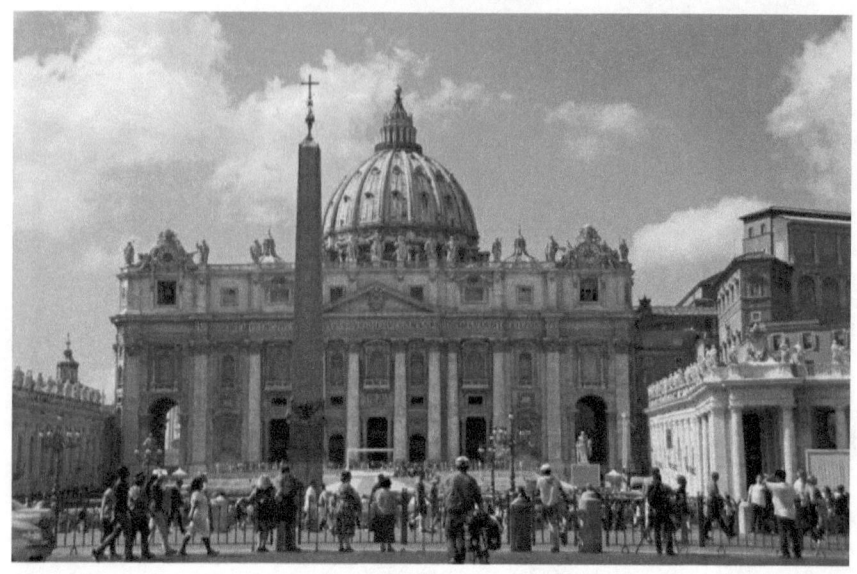

Tourists at St Peter's Basilica, Rome, Italy

Try to take in seasonal exhibits

Most major museums have rotating seasonal exhibits that either showcase travelling displays of art and artifacts, or that showcase treasures from the normal museum collection that are not normally on display. Thus, you should take advantage of seasonal exhibits to see stuff you otherwise couldn't. Museum curators often put in more effort to make seasonal exhibits entertaining in order to attract new guests, so you can be sure that seasonal exhibits will often take advantage of cutting-edge technology or lean into a hot-topic issue in order to get people in the door and be more exciting in the process. As well, part of the joy of travel is its transience, the fact that you cannot replicate the unique experience you're having in that specific part of the world at that specific part of your life, so embrace the transience with exhibits that won't be there forever either.

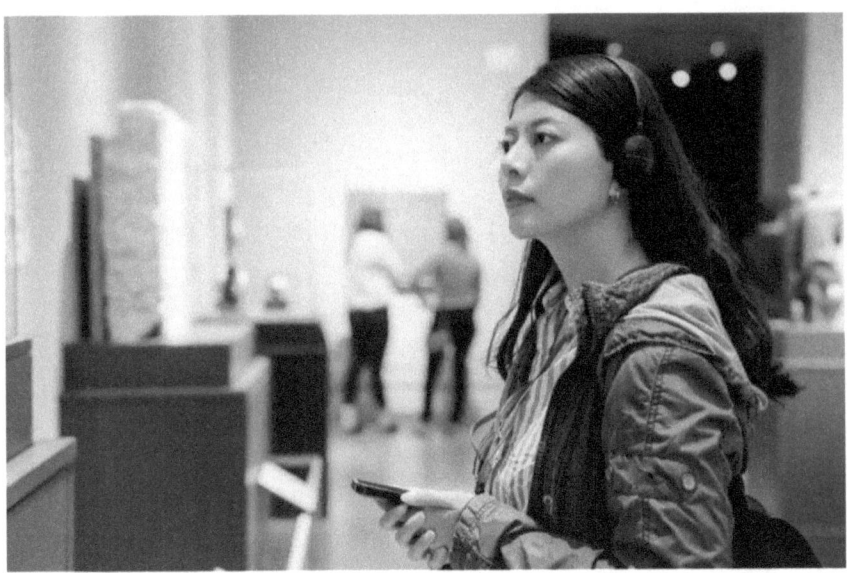

Read about the exhibit beforehand

You'll learn things in a museum, but never to the detail that you think you might before you visit. That's why you should learn about whatever the subject is beforehand. Heading to the Rijksmuseum in Amsterdam? Read a bit about the lives of Rembrandt and Vermeer so that you'll better appreciate their masterworks. Going to the Egyptian Museum in Cairo? If you know the broad strokes of which pharaohs ruled Egypt at what time periods, you'll enjoy seeing their elaborate tombs much more. As well, if you've already put the legwork in ahead of time to cultivate interest in the subjects on display in museums, the museums themselves will be infinitely more interesting. So it's a win-win approach to a museum visit.

Hieroglyphics display in Egyptian Museum, Cairo, Egypt

How to approach museum tours

Book a private tour ahead of time

If you're going to take a tour, plan it ahead of time so that it's entirely shaped around your interests. As well, opt for a private tour so that you'll enjoy personal attention throughout your entire museum visit. I know that private tours are more expensive, but there is nothing more likely to drain your interest in a museum than having to suffer through interminable questions from other travellers on a larger tour or having to spend extra time at some part of the exhibit you aren't interested in, but others are. Thus, if you go for a private tour, you'll do without the boring questions from other travellers. As well, your guide will shape the tour around your interests, meaning that you'll stay interested throughout your visit.

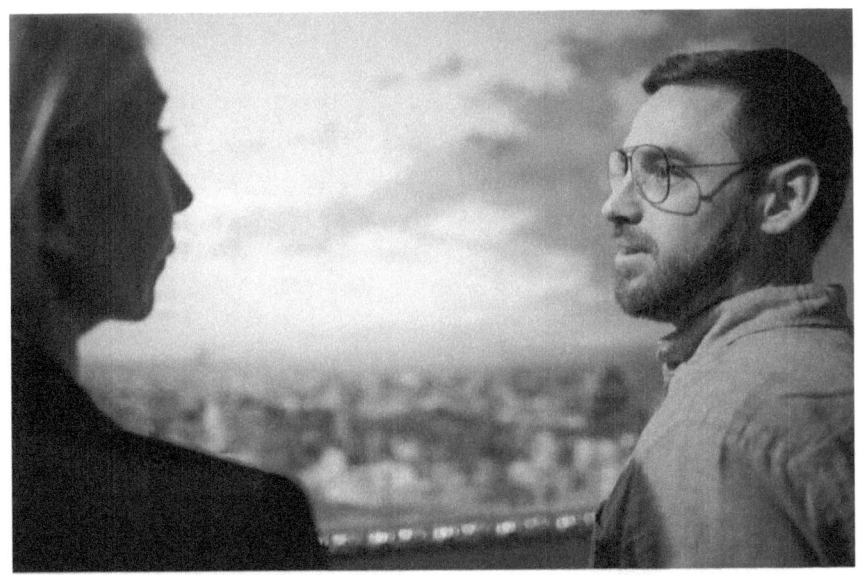

Or skip the tour altogether

I am not a fan of museum tours, so I am one of those travellers who is likely to skip the tour altogether and explore on my own. Back in the day, I was scared of missing out on details about the tour, but I realized that I preferred moving at my own pace and following my own fancy. What interests the tour guide might not interest me and over time, I've become more comfortable to simply head to parts of the museum that sound interesting and while away the hours exploring on my own. For instance, I love the Musee d'Orsay in Paris, but I spent most of my time looking at the Van Gogh, Monet, and Manet paintings and ignoring the many sculptures on display, as I love Impressionism and Post-Impression far more than other art styles. I may not have seen everything the museum has to offer, but I got to spend time on what I most cared about, so I don't regret striking out on my own and paying exclusive attention to my own interests.

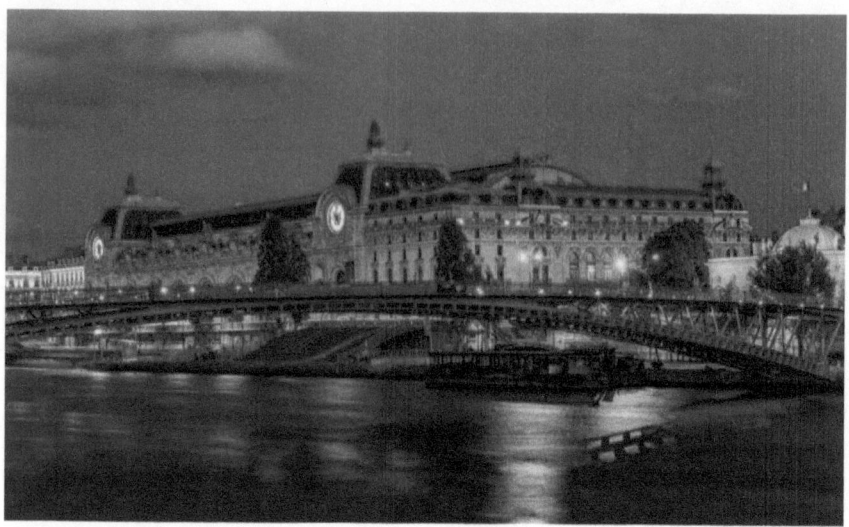

Orsay Museum (Musee d'Orsay) in Paris at night, France

What to do when visiting a museum

Lose the phone

No one wants to visit a museum while other people are livestreaming on Instagram or Snapchat, so don't be the person to do that yourself. As well, part of the appeal of museums are that they transport you to the past. However useful they are in everyday life, phones distract from this atmosphere. They pull you out of the past and constantly force you to pay attention to the present. So leave the phone in your purse or pocket and pay attention to the treasures on display. Who knows: you may even realize that what you're seeing was made by people with technology far more primitive than what you have in your purse or pocket, making it all the more impressive.

Don't take pictures

This is kind of an addendum to the previous point. Leave your phone in your pocket, meaning avoid taking pictures. This seems to go against everything about travel in the modern world, especially travel in the age of Instagram, which is all about making people jealous of the experiences you're having while on vacation (or selling a product, or both). But being in a museum is not the same as being at Machu Picchu or outside the Taj Mahal. Usually, taking a photo will not enhance the experience in a museum, and you'll almost never want to go back and look at photos you took in museums. (The big exception is if the photo is of the museum itself. Many museums are architectural attractions in their own right, and if that's the case of the museum you're visiting, shoot away!)

As well, a selfie will do little more than prove you were there, which you were, so why document it? Also keep in mind that all the artifacts on display will be recorded online, whether on the museum website itself or in other databases, archives, and general records. That photo you take of the Mona Lisa at the Louvre will never be as good as the official picture of the painting that you can find online. So leave your phone alone and pay attention to the work itself instead of obsessively documenting every moment. You'll have a more stress-free and patient experience by doing so.

Mother and daughter exploring expositions of previous centuries in museum

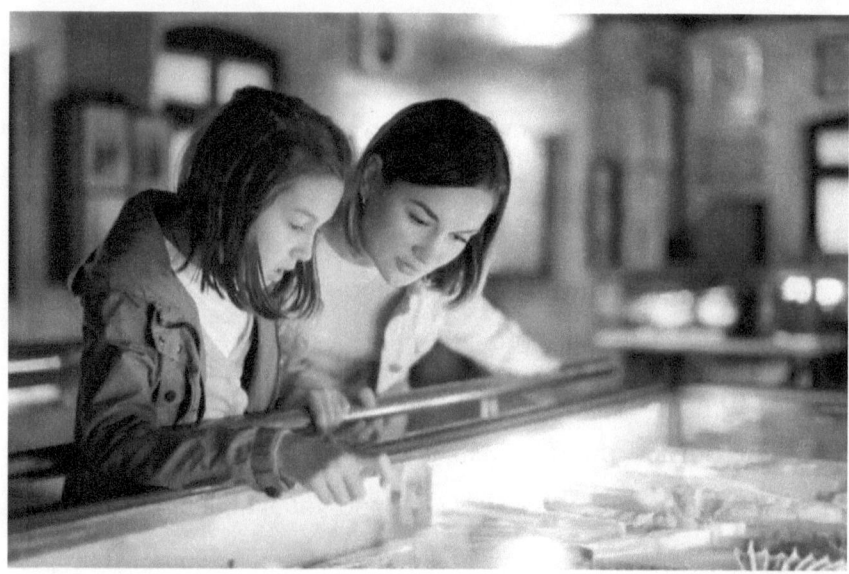

Get Obsessed with Details

Some people want to see everything when they visit a museum, but such an approach is a fool's errand. For instance, if you were to spend a minute looking at every painting on display in the Vatican Museums, you'd be there for several years. So slow down the pace, forget about seeing everything, and pay attention to the details. When looking at Van Gogh's Starry Night Over the Rhone, pay attention to the brush strokes and the thick layers of paint on the canvas. Spend 20 minutes staring at Rembrandt's The Night Watch, marvelling over how he was able to capture such palpable darkness in the frame. Stand back and really let the scale of Raphael's The School of Athens sink in. Appreciate the attention to detail in the character's faces and the depth of the scene. The more you pay attention, the more you'll appreciate what treasures these museums truly have. And the more you'll want to head to museums to see these artistic treasures up close.

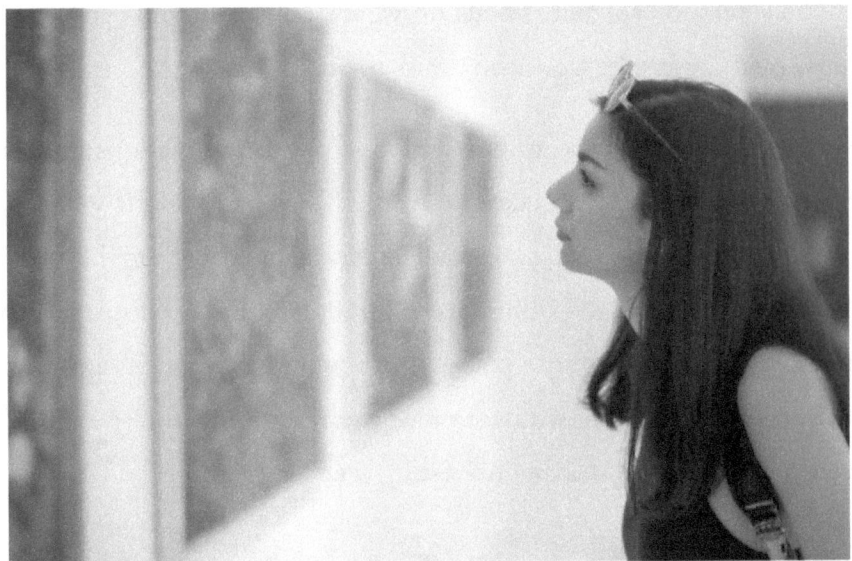

Skip the Café and Gift Shop

I like a coffee table book and latte as much as the next person, but museum gift shops and cafés are tourist traps that are overly crowded and expensive. Some museums have great restaurants in them that are the exception to this rule (like the Larco Museum in Lima), but for the most part, avoid the café unless you absolutely need a drink (staying hydrated is important), but always remember museums have water fountains that are free as well. As for the gift shop, all the pretty images in coffee table books are available online and you can often buy the books elsewhere for cheaper prices if you really do want them. Gift shops also have a way of making you spend more time in them than you want to; there's a reason the exit is always through the gift shop. So you may be tired and want to head to dinner, but dawdling in the gift shop has suddenly made you 30 minutes behind schedule. Focus on what's important and leave these spots by the wayside. You won't miss them.

Museums will always be among the most popular attractions in great cities of the world. So make the most of a museum visit when on vacation, knowing what you're interested in and how to best take advantage of the huge exhibitions of art and history on display. They may not be your favourite places in the world, but if you approach them correctly and know how to navigate them once you're in, you'll have a much more positive, interesting time.

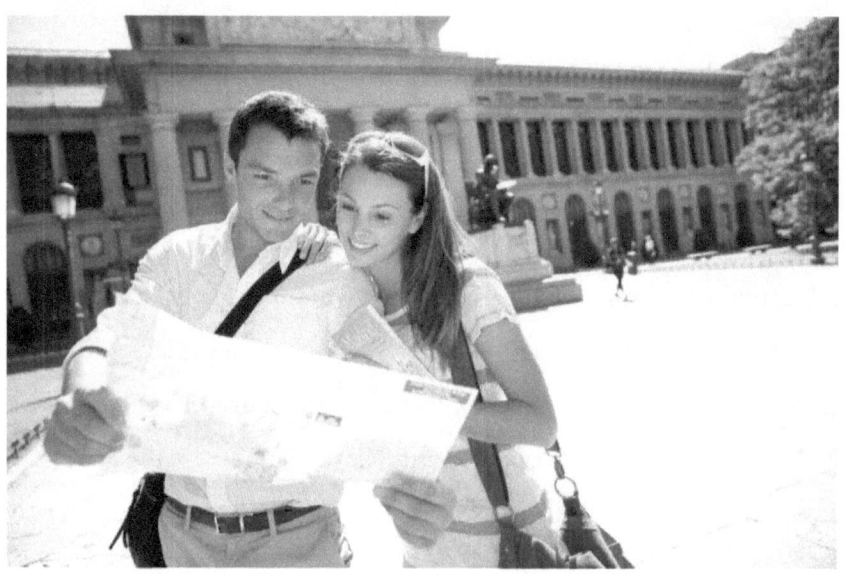

If you're interested in getting the most out of museum visits, plan your trip with the help of a destination expert who'll help you follow your interests in great cities around the globe.

Best Museums

in the World

Museum of Black Civilizations in Dakar, Senegal

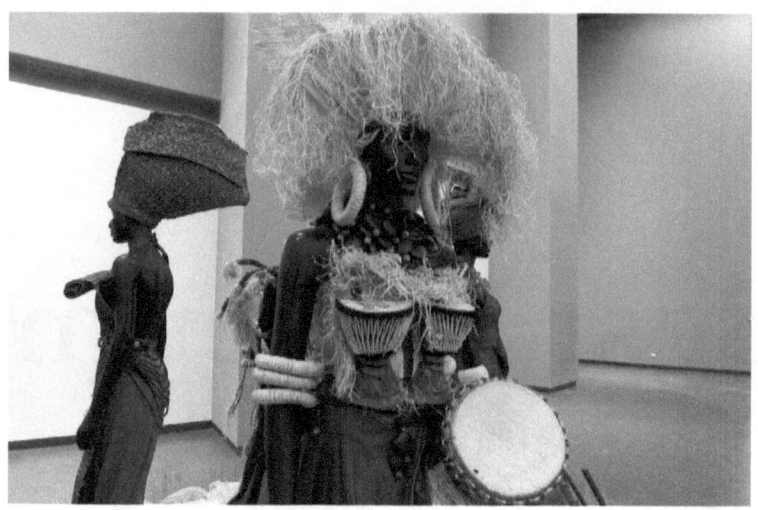

Inaugurated in 2018, the Museum of Black Civilizations acts as a creative hub for Senegal—and the entire African continent—to celebrate their culture while detailing the struggle that Africans faced throughout history. The museum was the vision of the country's first president Léopold Sédar Senghor, who vowed to build an institution honoring African art and identity. While Senghor unfortunately passed before the museum opened, his legacy lives on in the curated art selections and striking displays filling the galleries.

The opening of the cultural landmark also spurred a debate amongst the art world, with many scholars calling for museums throughout Europe to return thousands of artifacts looted from Africa during the colonial period.

Museum of the Royal Tombs of Sipán in Chiclayo, Peru

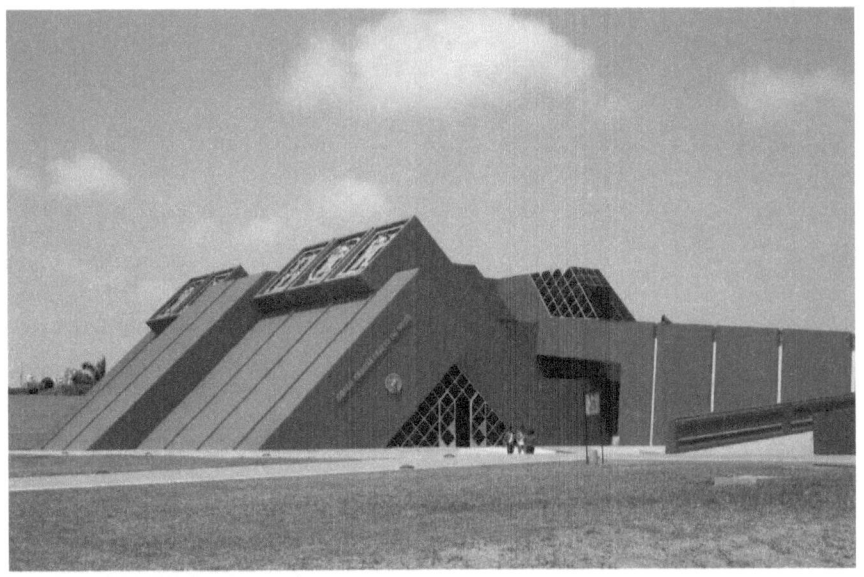

In 1987, Peruvian archaeologist Walter Alva was called upon by police to investigate the Moche archaeological site at Sipán, where grave robbers had been looting artifacts. When he began excavating the site, Alva soon found he was not unearthing a few pieces of jewelry and gold, but rather, the tombs of the Lord of Sipán and 14 other members of the Moche civilization.

The Museum of the Royal Tombs of Sipán was built to honor and display what has been considered one of the most important archaeological discoveries in South America. Guests can ogle lavish jewels, regal vessels, and other stunning artifacts of Peru's ancient community.

Bangkok National Museum

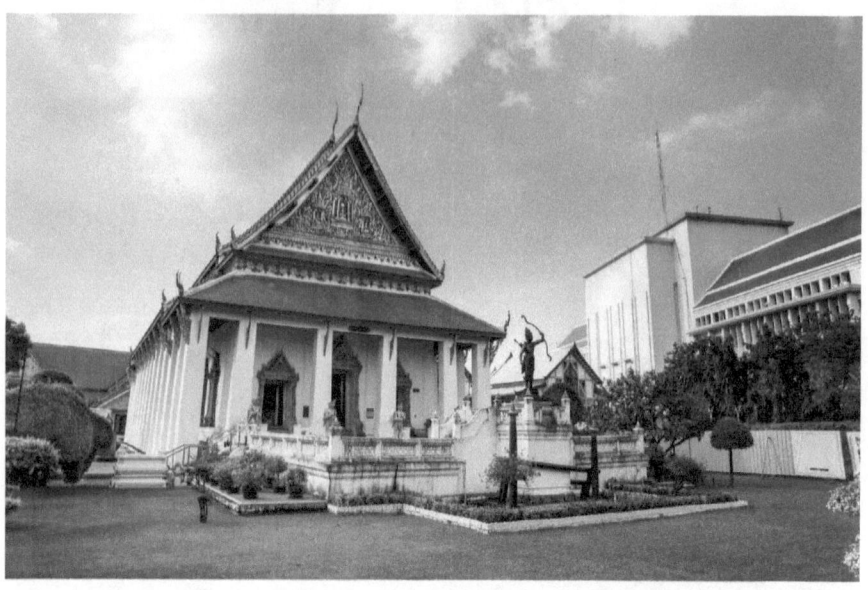

The first national museum in Thailand, this Bangkok cultural splendor houses the country's most extensive collection of Thai artifacts and artwork. The museum's structures can be traced back to 1782, when they served as the palace of Rama I's viceroy, Prince Wang Na.

Nearly 100 years later, the grounds were transformed into a museum with three differently themed galleries: a Thai History Gallery, an Archaeological and Art History collection, and a Decorative Arts and Ethnological Collection. In addition to the main collections, guests can discover one of the most revered images of Buddha, Phra Phuttha Sihing, in the Bhuddhaisawan Chapel.

The National Art Center in Tokyo

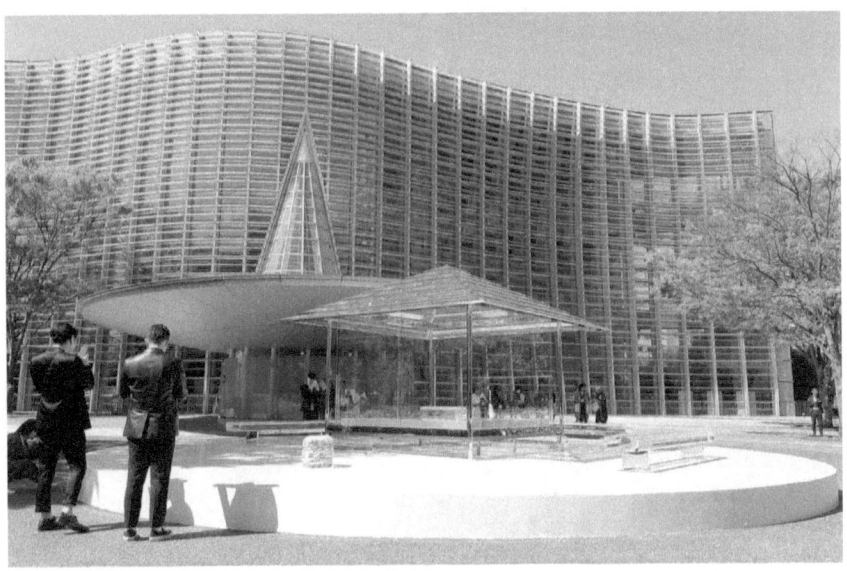

You never quite know what awe-striking sculpture or Japanese masterpiece you'll find at this impressive institution. The National Art Center prides itself in being an "empty museum," constantly ushering new exhibitions and collections spread across it's concrete-and-glass structure designed by Kisho Kurokawa.

Established in 2007, the quirky museum quickly grew in popularity and became a must-see attraction in Tokyo, boasting roughly 2 million visitors each year. Past exhibitions cover a wide range of topics from the Impressionist works of Claude Monet and the impact of anime on Japanese culture to the history of Cartier.

National Museum of African American History and Culture in Washington, D.C.

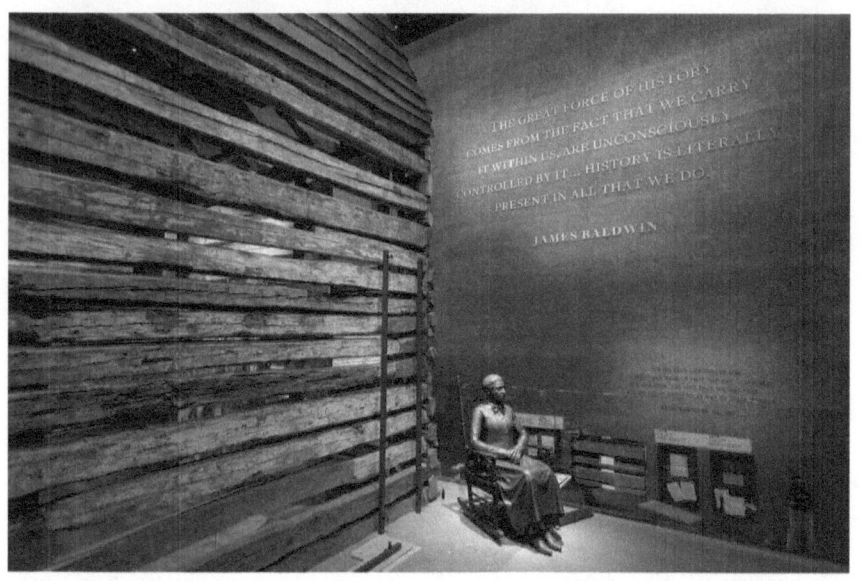

The only national museum devoted to the documentation of the African American experience, this Smithsonian institution was inaugurated in 2016. However, the idea of the museum was first proposed more than a hundred years before in 1915 by Black veterans of the Civil War. The initial proposal called for a monument to be erected in the honor of Black soldiers and sailors in the nation's capital, but debates over funding and site locations kept pushing the project back.

It wasn't until 2003 when an Act of Congress established the institution and construction plans began. Today, the National Museum of African American History and Culture houses more than 40,000 objects dedicated to African American life, history, and culture.

Zeitz Museum of Contemporary Art Africa in Cape Town

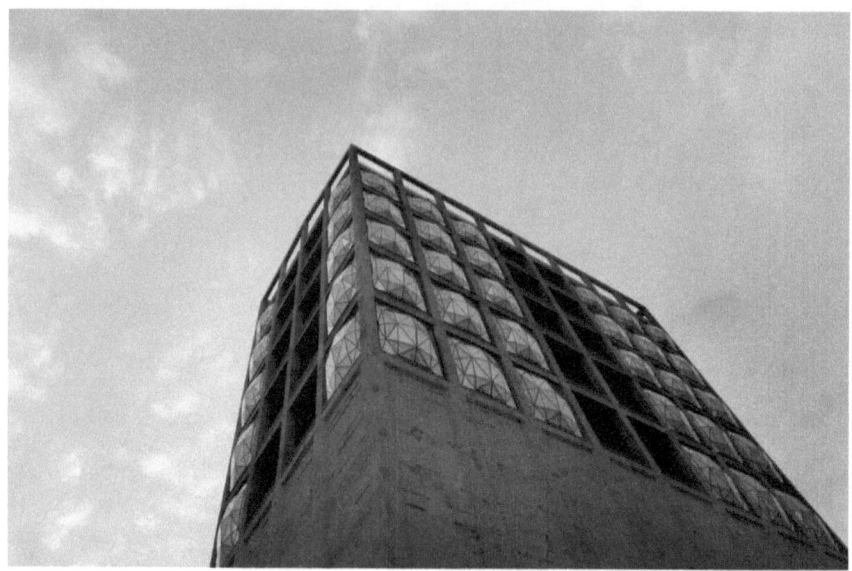

With the help of design firm Heatherwick Studio, the once-magnolia-yellow, century-old grain silo complex in the heart of Cape Town transformed into a 100-gallery museum of 21st-century art from Africa and its diaspora. Zeitz MOCAA hosts international events and exhibitions to provide an intercultural look into the world of African art. Works from revolutionary artists such as Kudzanai Chiurai of Zimbabwe and Wangechi Mutu of Kenya decorate the nine floors of the museum.

National Gallery of Canada in Ottawa

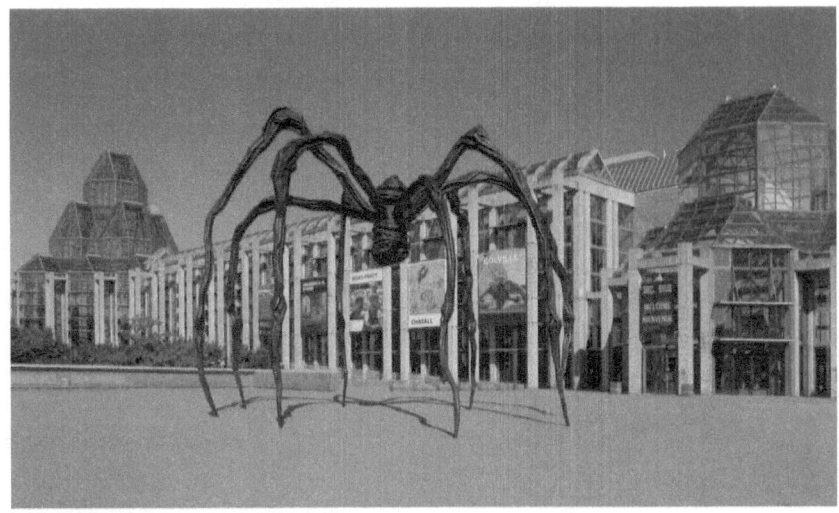

When the National Gallery of Canada was established in 1880, the first exhibition primarily consisted of 19th-century works at the historic Clarendon Hotel in Ottawa. Over 140 years later, a 30-foot bronze spider called the Maman greets visitors at the gallery's new home designed by architect Moshe Safdie.

The national art museum now houses 75,000 works of art ranging from Canadian and Indigenous pieces to the neoclassicist painting The Death of General Wolfe by Benjamin West.

Tate Modern in London

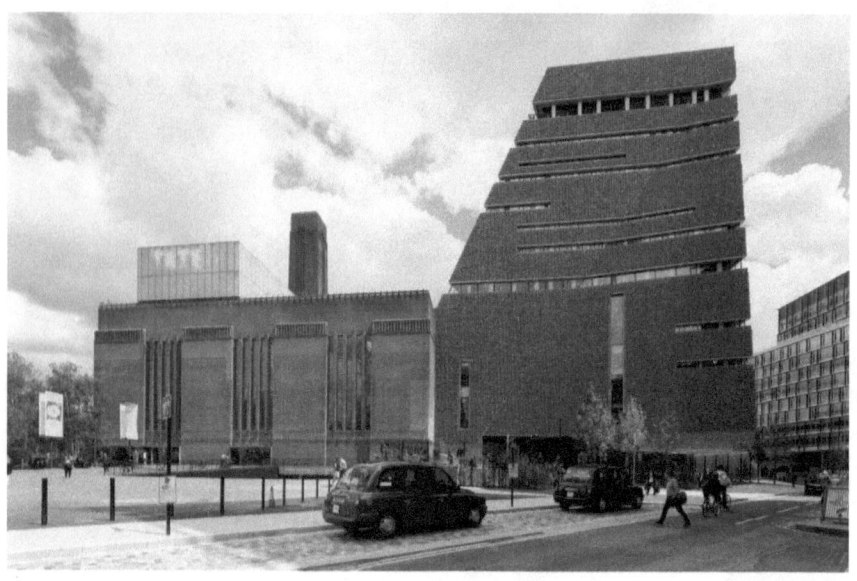

The birth of Tate Modern began in 1889 when Henry Tate, a British industrialist, donated his collection of British 19th-century art and provided funding for the first Tate Gallery. A century later, the Tate Trustees announced the development of an international modern and contemporary art gallery.

Located within the former Bankside Power Station, the gallery showcases groundbreaking works including Marilyn Diptych by Andy Warhol and Nude Woman with Necklace by Pablo Picasso.

The Metropolitan Museum of Art in New York City

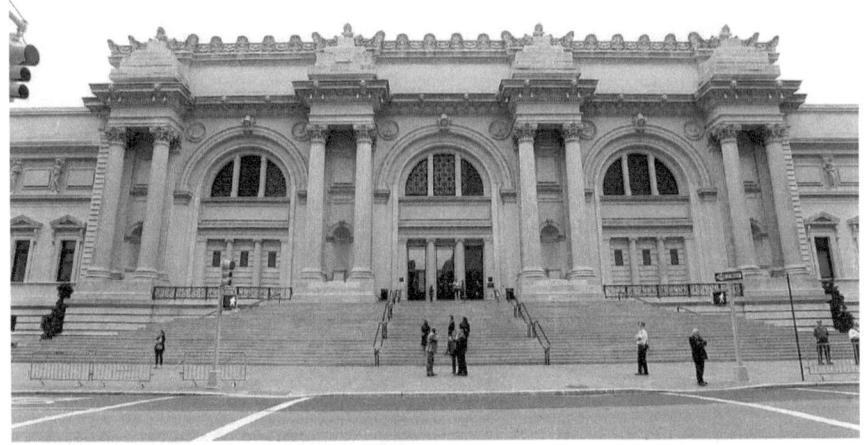

The beginnings of the Metropolitan Museum of Art date back as far as 1866 in Paris, France, where a group of Americans discussed the need to bring art education to the public. On April 13, 1870, the Met opened within the historic Dodworth Building before moving to its permanent location on Fifth Avenue and 82nd Street in 1880.

The museum presents over 5,000 years of artwork, including Islamic art dating back to the seventh century and the well-known Edgar Degas' painting The Dance Class.

Mauritshuis in The Hague, Netherlands

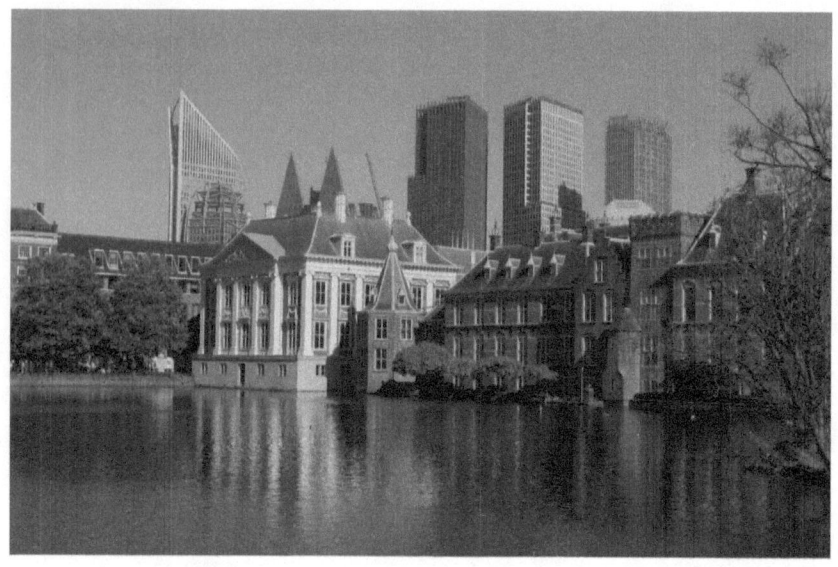

Known as the Royal Picture Gallery of the Netherlands, Mauritshuis houses a rare collection of Golden Age paintings from countless Dutch and Flemish artisans. In 1816, King William I offered the collections once owned by his father, stadtholder Prince William V, to the Dutch state, establishing the first national gallery in The Hague. The Mauritshuis's 841 works of art include Johannes Vermeer's Girl with a Pearl Earring and Carel Fabritius' The Goldfinch.

The National Palace Museum in Taipei

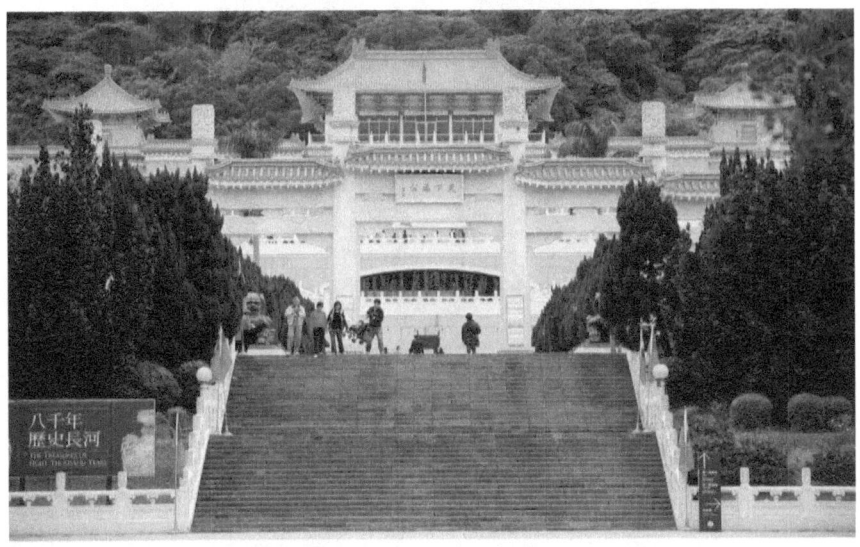

The National Palace Museum originally began as the former Palace Museum in the Forbidden City, whose collection included artwork from the Ming and Qing dynasties. The permanent collection features nearly 700,000 pieces of imperial artifacts and encompasses 8,000 years of Chinese history including calligraphic works by Tang Yin. The National Palace Museum compound also includes the classic Chinese Song- and Ming-style Zhishan Garden.

The Museum of Egyptian Antiquities in Cairo

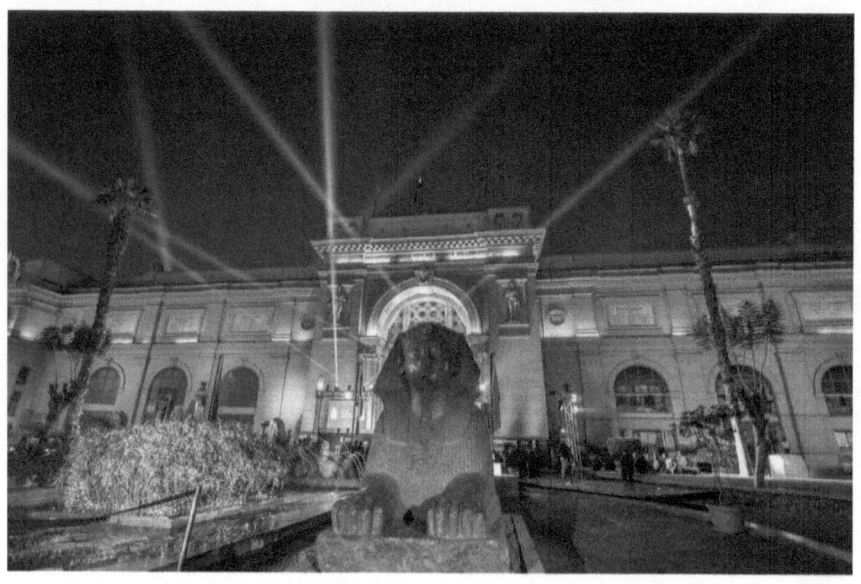

One of the largest museums in North Africa, the Egyptian Museum houses nearly 120,000 ancient Egyptian artifacts and the world's largest collection of Pharaonic antiquities. The museum was commissioned in 1835 by the Egyptian government in hopes to stop the looting of many archeological and historic sites. Visitors can come face-to-face with the gold mask of Tutankhamun, which is composed of 11 kilograms of solid gold.

Kunsthistorisches Museum in Vienna

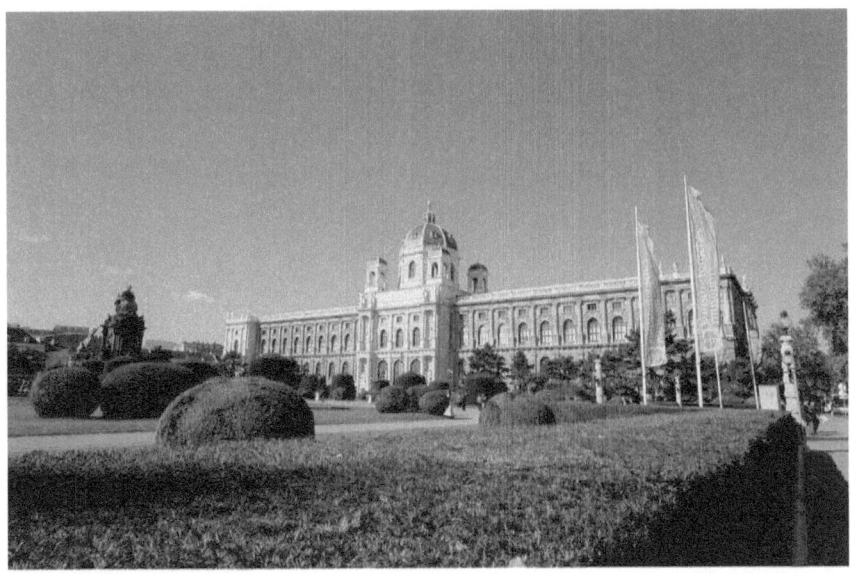

Emperor Franz Joseph I of Austria-Hungary commissioned the Kunsthistorisches Museum around 1891 as a place to display the terrific art collection from the House of Hapsburgs, which is the still the museum's primary collection. Housed within the palatial building on Ringstraße, the museum's works includes Madonna del Prato by Raphael and Diego Velázquez's well-known portrait Infanta Margarita Teresa in a Blue Dress.

Museo de Arte de Puerto Rico

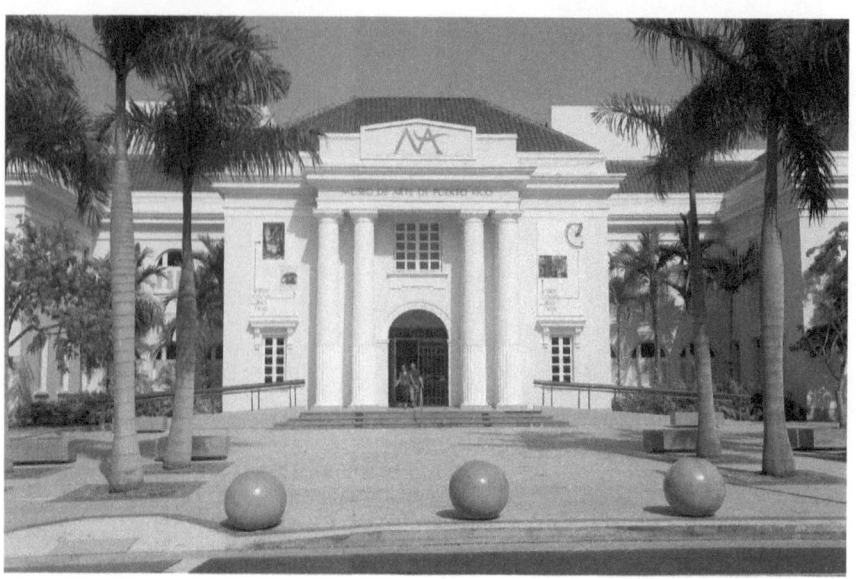

Inaugurated in 2000, Museo de Arte de Puerto Rico's mission is to promote visual arts from Puerto Rico and around the world to a diverse audience. The museum's primary and expansive collection of Puerto Rican art ranges from the 16th century to the present. The museum includes pieces such as Chula (Girl in typical Madrid Costume) by José Cuchy y Arnau and the 18th-century work The Daughters of Governor Ramón de Castro by José Campeche.

The San Francisco Museum of Modern Art

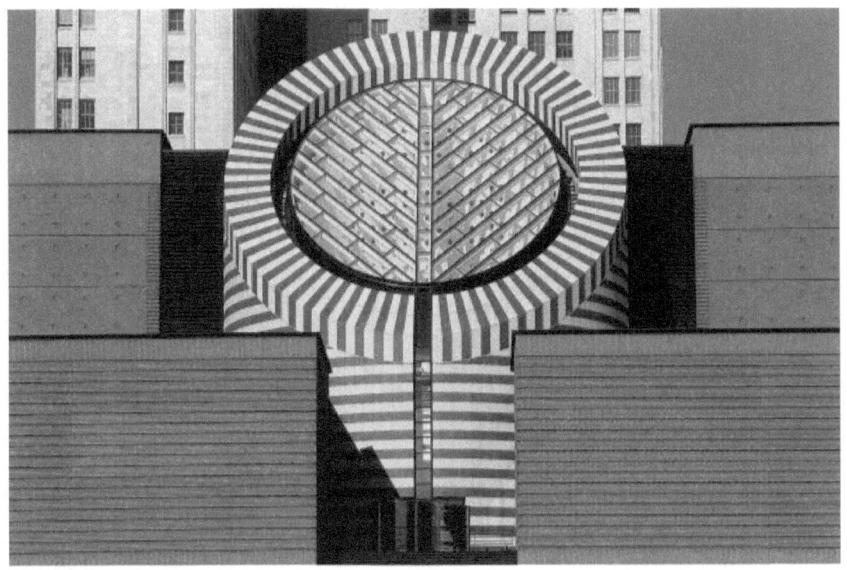

The first museum on the West Coast devoted solely to 20th-century art since 1935, the San Francisco Museum of Modern Art boasts an impressive seven floors of galleries with over 33,000 works and a wall seeded with thousands of plants. SFMoMA holds some of the most internationally recognizable modern art pieces including Henri Matisse's Woman with a Hat and Marcel Duchamp's provocative Fountain.

Museo Nacional de Antropología in Mexico City

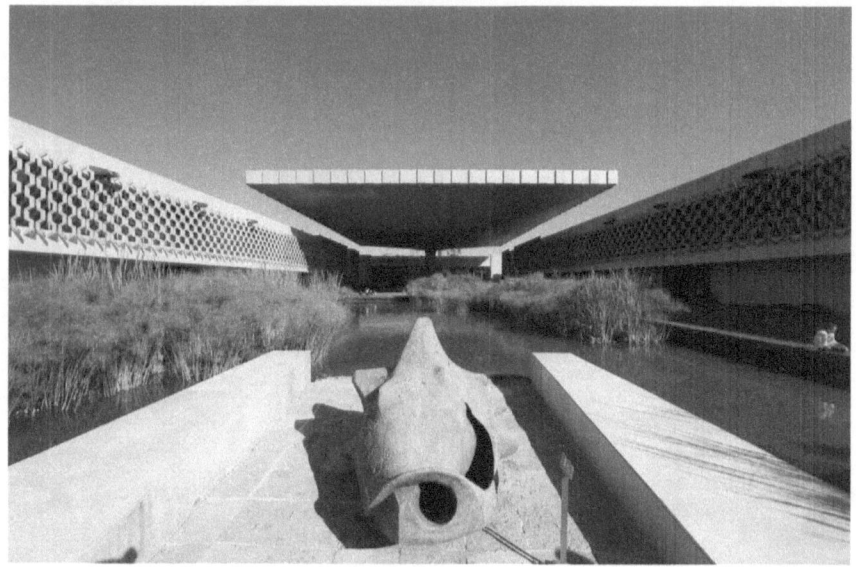

The largest and most visited museum in Mexico, Museo Nacional de Antropología specializes in the history of the country's pre-Columbian heritage through archaeological artifacts. Architect Pedro Ramírez Vázquez paid tribute to the indigenous legacy of Mexico by building the museum in the Chapultepec Forest, emphasizing a natural relationship with the environment. The 600,000-piece collection includes the Aztec Stone of Sun and the Xochipilli statue.

Musée D'Orsay in Paris

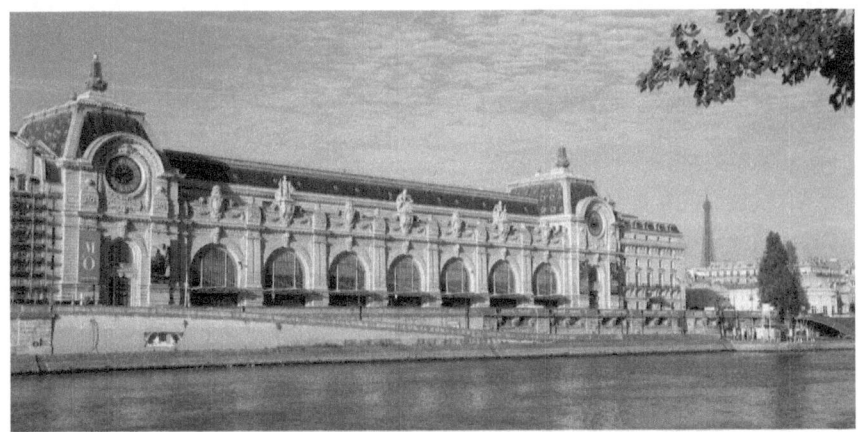

The Musée D'Orsay, once a railway station, houses an internationally renowned collection of Impressionist art and other Western pieces from 1848 and 1914. Architect Victor Laloux built the original magnificent structure in 1900 to welcome visitors to the World's Fair. After its closure in 1939, the Beaux-Arts station remained in a state of disuse until President Valery Giscard authorized renovations on the historic building in the late 1970s.

Inaugurated in 1986, the white limestone walls are now home to some of the most notable artworks in France, like sculptures by Auguste Rodin and paintings by Paul Gauguin.

The Art Institute of Chicago

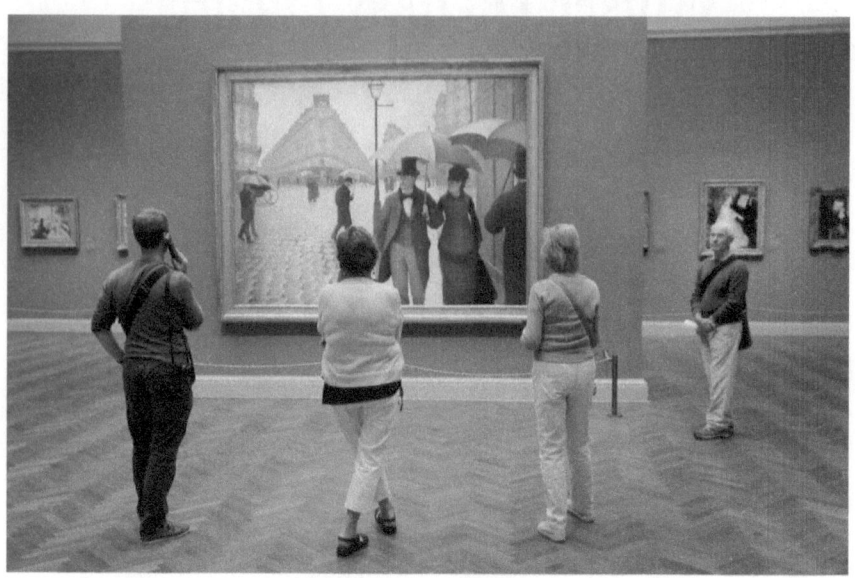

The Art Institute of Chicago has over 300,000 works of art for visitors to view across the original building and the Modern Wing designed by Renzo Piano. After the Great Fire of 1871, Chicago leaders were devoted to rebuilding and growing the city, which included opening a museum and school for the fine arts.

The Art Institute found its permanent home at the corner of Michigan Avenue and Adams Street in 1893 with two bronze lions marking the front entrance of the museum. Gustave Caillebotte's Paris Street; Rainy Day and Grant Wood's American Gothic are among the Institute's massive collection.

Museo Larco in Lima

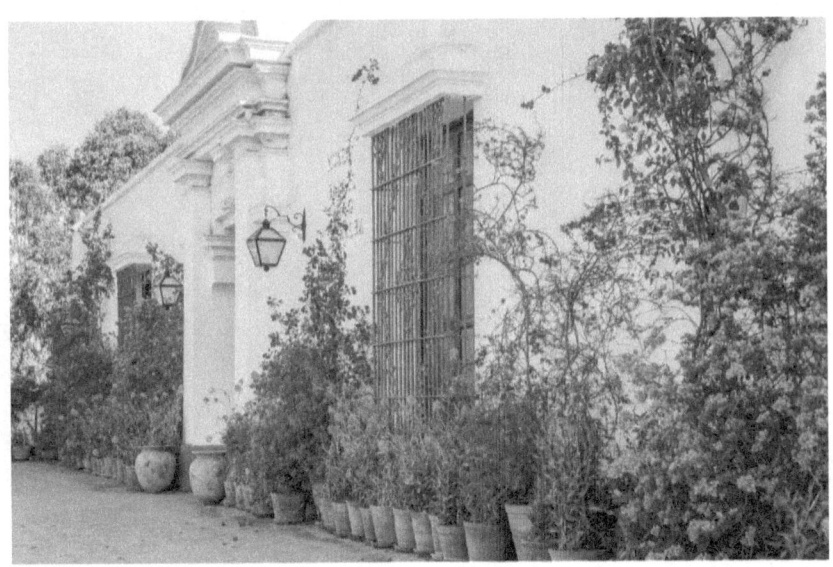

Located in the Pueblo Libre District of Lima, Museo Larco specializes in pre-Columbian art, spanning over 5,000 years of Peruvian history. Established by Rafael Larco Hoyle in 1926 after acquiring 45,000 artifacts and vessels, the institution is currently housed in an 18th-century vice-royal building. Among the museum's permanent collection, the Gold and Silver Gallery displays the largest collection of pre-Columbian jewelry, which was often worn by notable rulers during that time.

The Museum of Qin Terracotta Warriors and Horses in Xi'an, China

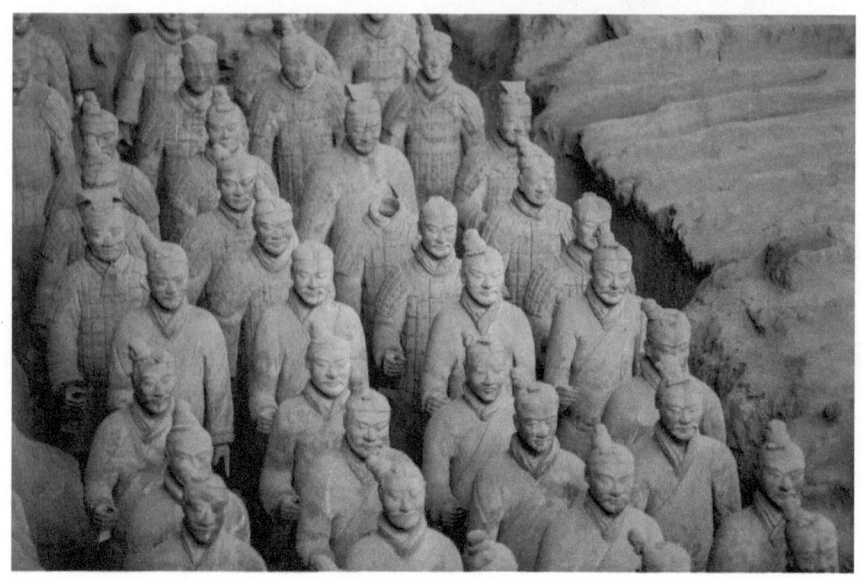

The ancient Chinese funerary art of terra-cotta sculptures at this mausoleum and museum depicts the armies of Qin Shi Huang, the first Emperor of China. The terra-cotta army, dating back to the late third century, was discovered by local farmers in 1974 just outside of Xi'an City. It's estimated that the three pits within the mausoleum contains more than 8,000 soldiers, 130 chariots with 520 horses, and 150 cavalry horses. Within the same site, visitors can also enjoy the Museum of Terracotta Acrobatics, Museum of Terracotta Civil Officials, Museum of Stone Armor and Museum of Bronze Chariot and Horse.

The Musée du Louvre in Paris

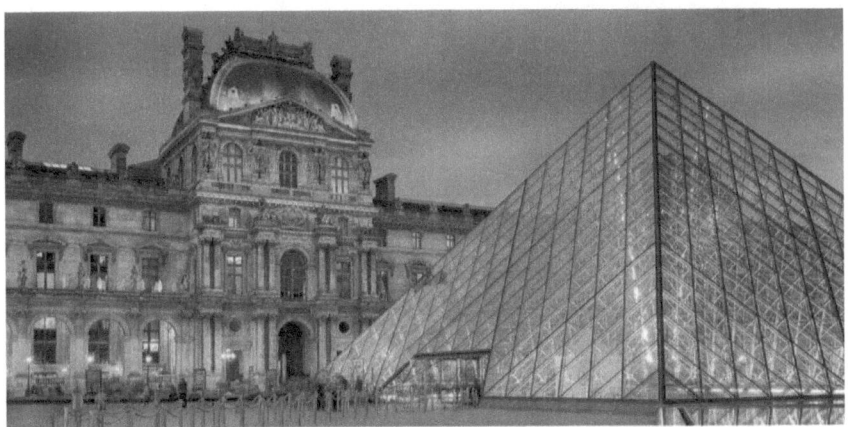

The Musée du Louvre has way more to offer than just Leonardo da Vinci's Mona Lisa. King Philip II ordered the construction of a fortress in 1190 to protect Paris. During the 16th century, the Louvre served as a royal palace for the monarchy until King Louis XIV moved the royal residence to Versailles. The National Assembly opened the Louvre as a museum in 1793, starting its legacy as the world's largest art museum. The Winged Victory of Samothrace and Psyche Revived by Cupid's Kiss are just a few of the nearly 380,000 works of art within the Louvre.

State Hermitage Museum in St. Petersburg

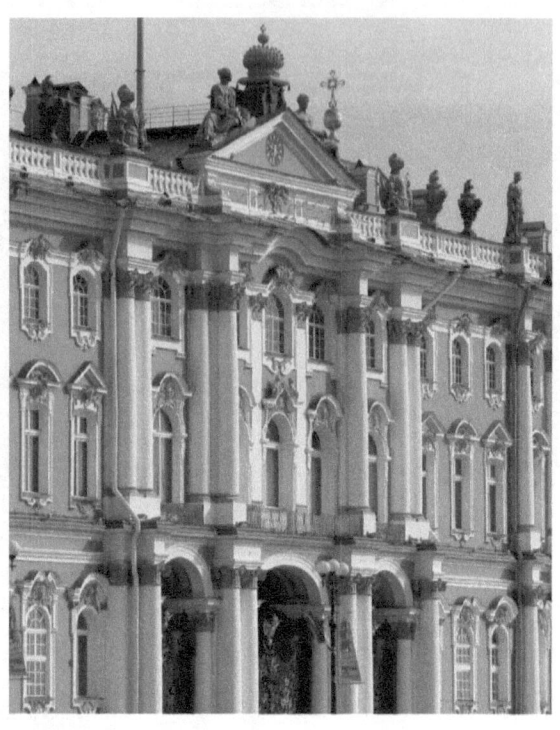

The State Hermitage Museum has roots dating back to 1764, after Catherine the Great wanted a private gallery within the Winter Palace to display her acquisition of 225 paintings by Flemish and Dutch artists. Today, the Hermitage Museum houses more than a million works of art and consists of five buildings—the Winter Palace, Large Hermitage, Small Hermitage, New Hermitage, and Theatre of Catherine the Great. The art and culture museum is home to a number of pieces by Dutch painter Rembrandt as well as an extensive collection of Japanese porcelain.

Museo Nacional Del Prado in Madrid

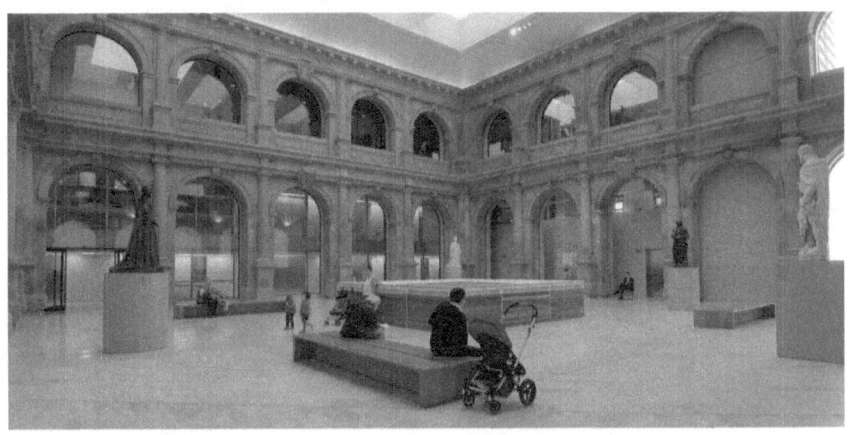

Designed by famed architect Juan de Villanueva, the Museo Nacional Del Prado serves as Spain's national museum, showcasing countless Spanish artists like Diego Velázquez and Francisco Goya. King Charles III ordered the construction of the Prado in 1785 to house the Natural History Cabinet.

King Ferdinand VII later designated the building as the new home of the Spain's most valuable paintings and sculptures in November of 1819. The Prado announced in 2016 that British architect Norman Foster and Carlos Rubio Carvajal will renovate the Hall of Realms, formerly a part of the Buen Retiro palace, as a $32 million extension to the museum.

The National Gallery in London

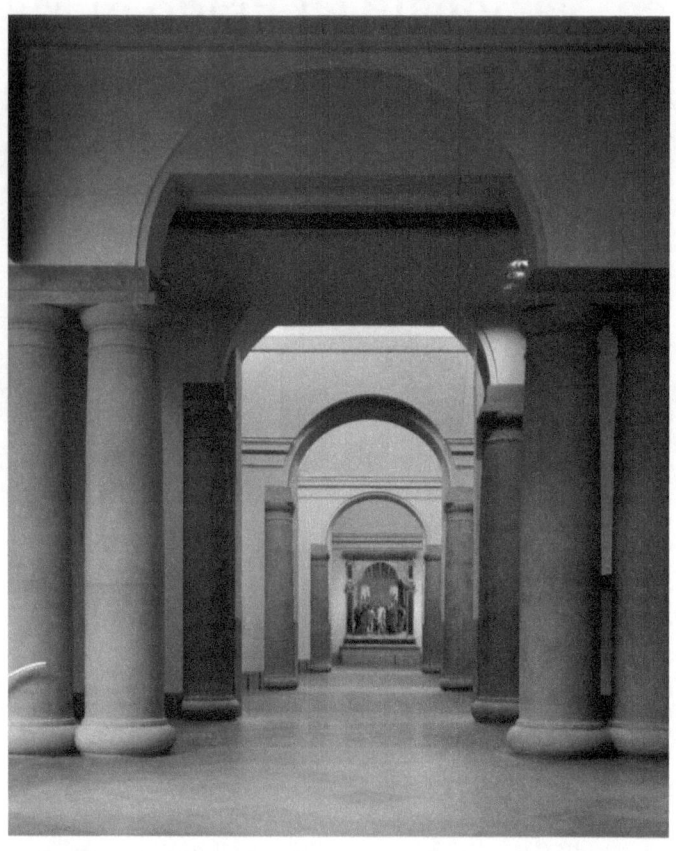

Located on the north side of Trafalgar Square, the National Gallery houses the national collection of Western European paintings from the 13th to the 19th centuries. Opened in 1838, parliament felt that Trafalgar Square would be the perfect location for a free museum for its central location, making it possible for people of all classes of society to easily access the paintings. The permanent collection includes The Arnolfini Portrait by Jan Van Eyck and The Great Bathers by Paul Cézanne.

Rijksmuseum in Amsterdam

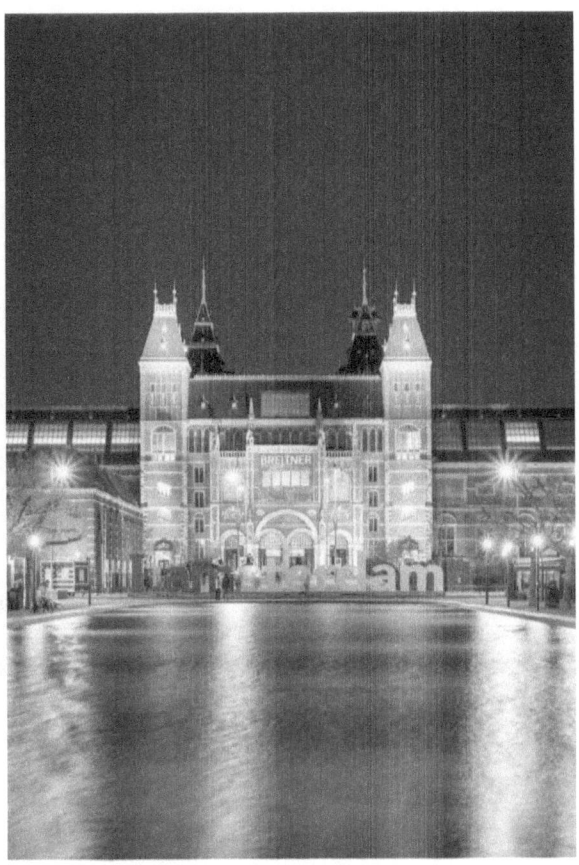

Formerly known as Nationale Kunstgalerij, Rijksmuseum first opened its doors on May 31, 1800, with more than 200 paintings and historical objects on display. Soon after taking the throne, King Louis Napoleon ordered that the collections be moved to the new capital of the Kingdom of Holland, Amsterdam, where it remains today.

The collection consists of one million objects dedicated to art and history with the museum's first purchase, The Swan by Jan Asselijn, remaining one of Rijksmuseum's most renowned pieces.

The Vasa Museum in Stockholm

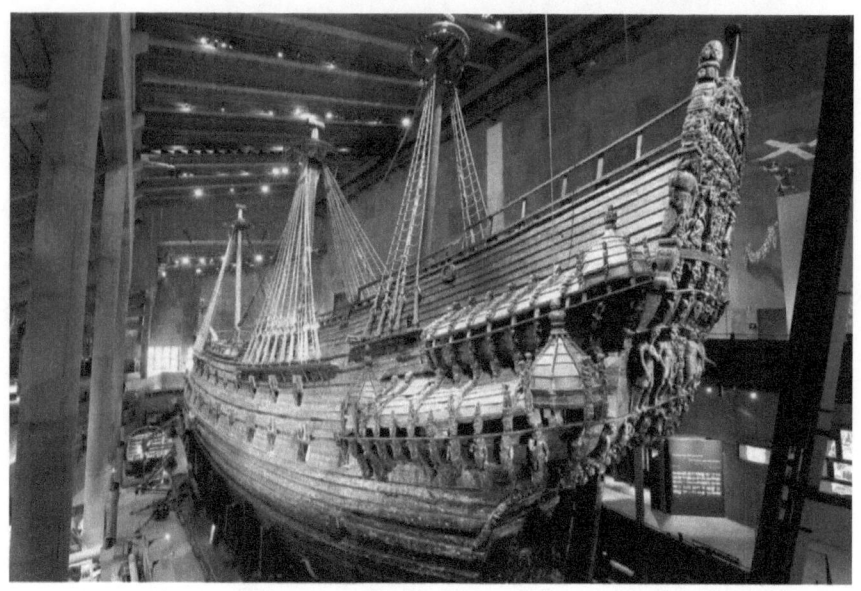

Board this recovered 17th-century Swedish ship for the ultimate trip down Scandinavian memory lane at the Vasa Museum. Gustav II Adolf lead the construction of new Swedish navy ships around 1618 including the Vasa, named after the Vasa Dynasty. The ship was regarded as one of the most powerful warships in the Baltic until it ultimately sunk in August of 1628. As a part of the museum today, the recovered ship is now embellished with hundreds of wooden sculptures.

The Acropolis Museum in Athens

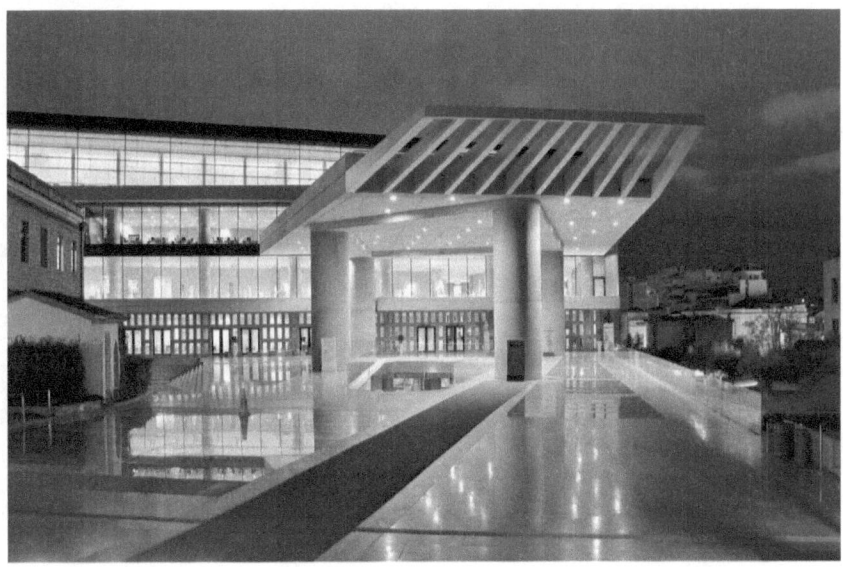

The highly curated exhibits of the Acropolis Museum focuses on the archaeological findings in the Acropolis of Athens between the Greek Bronze Age and Byzantine era. Located in the historic area of Makriyianni, the museum was founded in 1976 and houses nearly 4,000 sculptures and antiquities.

The British Museum in London

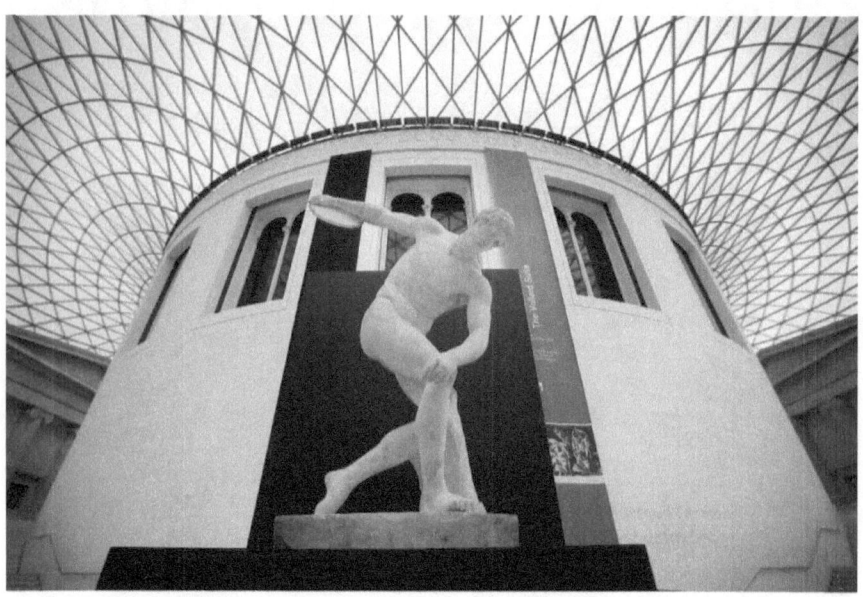

The first national museum in the world, the British Museum was established by parliament when physician Sir Hans Sloane passed on 71,000 items to King George II for the nation after his death in 1753. Sir Robert Smirke designed the museum's current Greek Revival-style building, including the famous copper-domed Reading Room. The museum also is the current holder of the classic Elgin Marbles and the Rosetta Stone.

The Van Gogh Museum in Amsterdam

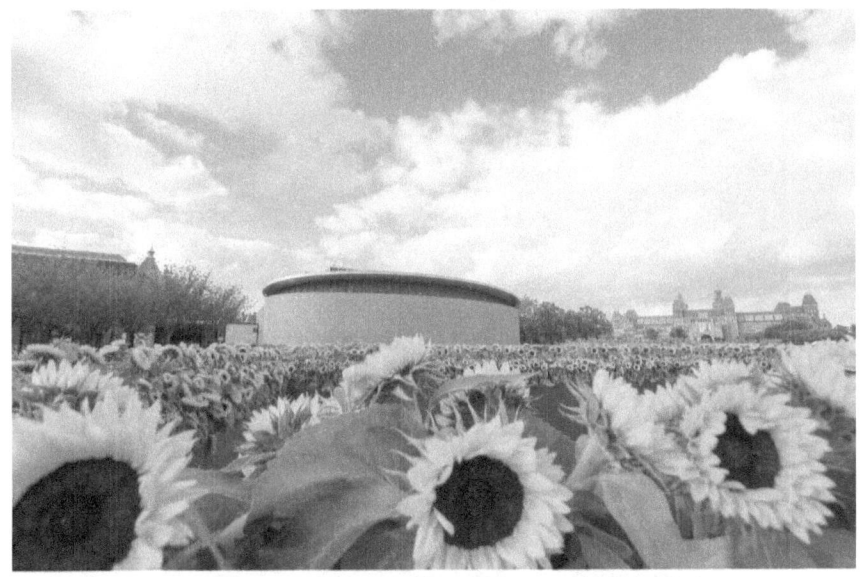

Touted as one of the most influential Dutch painters of all time, Vincent van Gogh produced nearly 900 paintings and more than 1,100 works on paper during his lifetime. The two buildings of the Vincent van Gogh Museum were designed by Gerrit Rietveld in 1973 with the core of the collection coming from Theo van Gogh, Vincent's younger brother. Along with his own artwork like Sunflowers, the gallery also includes work by those van Gogh influenced.

Galleria dell'Accademia in Florence

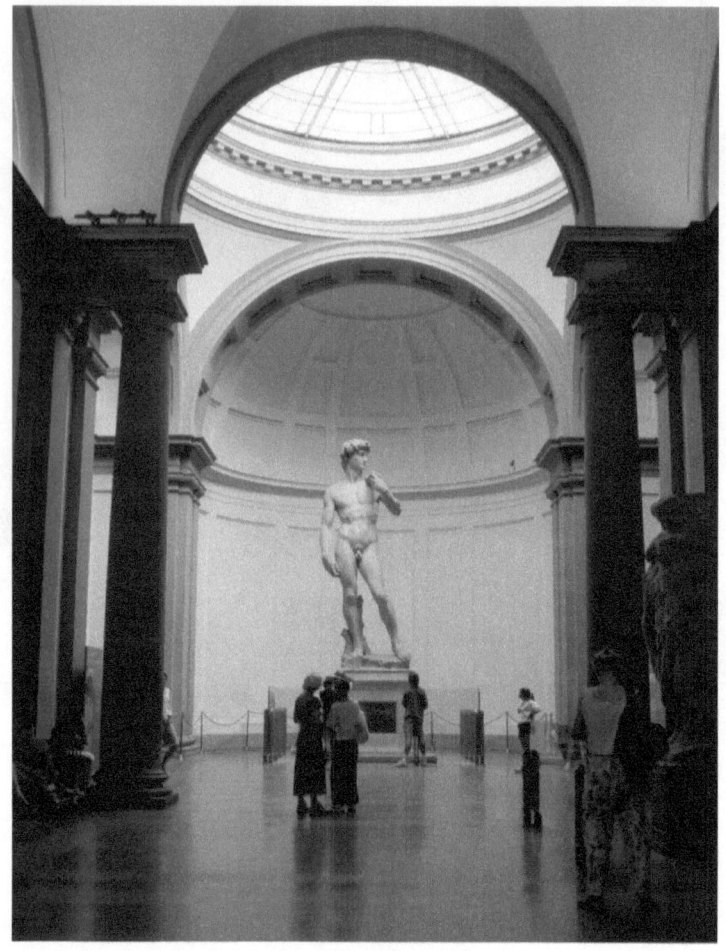

The Grand Duke of Tuscany established the Galleria dell'Accademia in the 18th-century as a teaching facility for students of the Academy of Fine Arts. Michelangelo's David joined the museum in 1873 from Piazza della Signoria, becoming the museum's must-see attraction. The Academia Gallery also showcases a collection of antic musical instruments.

The National WWII Museum in New Orleans

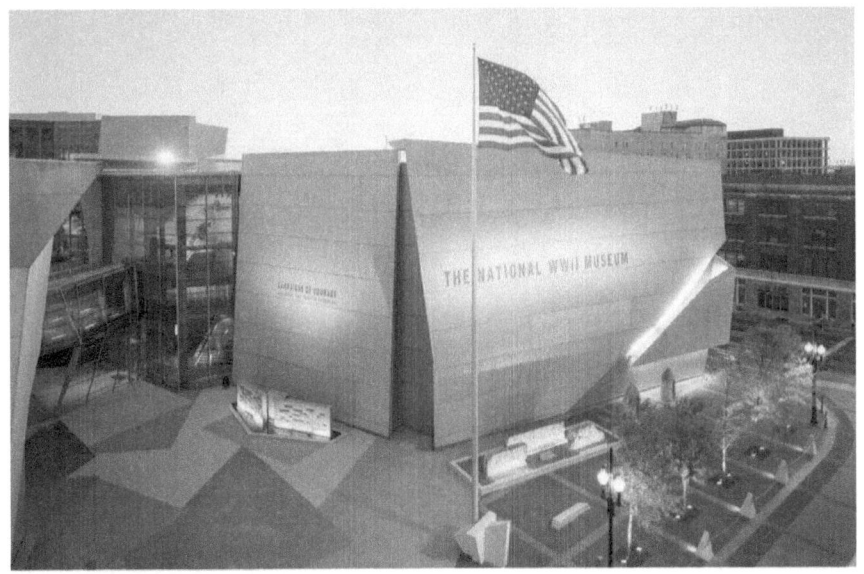

The National WWII Museum explains the grueling facts of the war—why it was fought, how it was won, and what it means today—from the American perspective. Two historians, Stephen Ambrose and Gordon H. "Nick" Mueller established the war museum in 2000, and it was later designated as America's National WWII Museum by a 2004 act of Congress. The grounds include five pavilions that house historical exhibits, on-site restoration work, a period dinner theater, and restaurants.

Pergamon Museum in Berlin

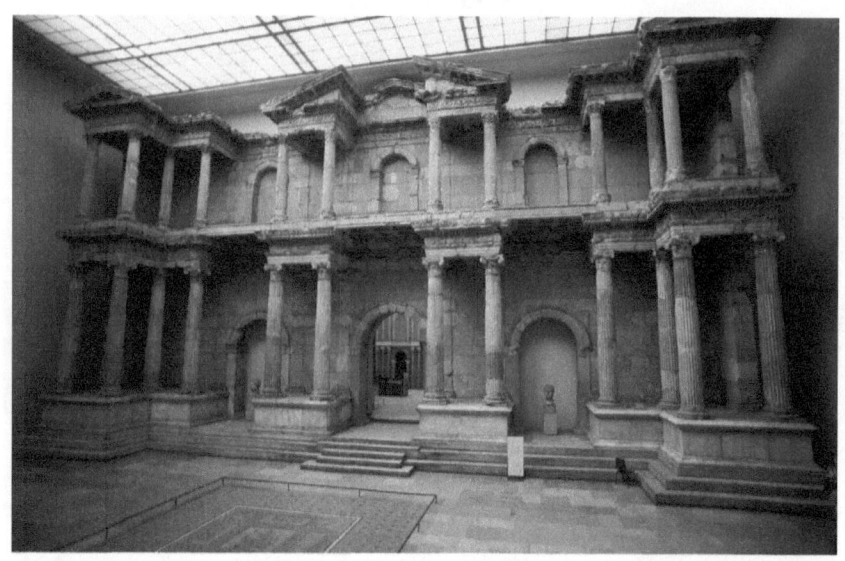

As the most-visited museum in Germany, the Pergamon houses reconstructions of massive archaeological structures like the Pergamon Altar, Market Gate of Miletus, the Ishtar Gate of Babylon, and the Mshatta Facade. During the 19th-century, the discovery of the ancient city of Troy by archaeologist Heinrich Schliemann fueled German researchers to travel to Babylon, Uruk, Ashur and Egypt to discover other worldly treasures. Museum Island become the location of preservation for these ancient treasures and later home to the Pergamon Museum.

The Getty Center in Los Angeles

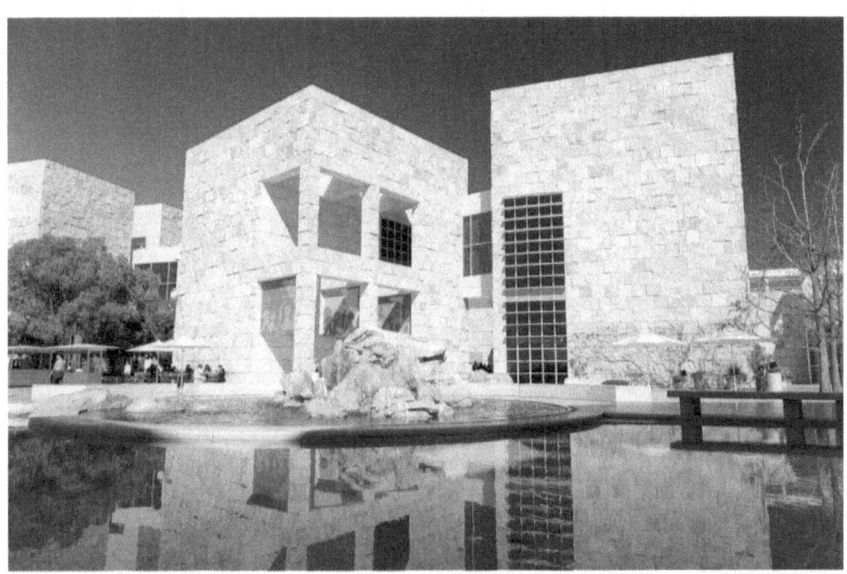

The Getty Center is the West Coast institution that hosts European paintings, drawings, sculpture, illuminated manuscripts, decorative arts, and photography. The origins of the Getty date back to 1953 when art collector J. Paul Getty established his own eponymous art trust and converted part of his ranch house into a museum. After his passing, the businessman left the vast bulk of his estate to the J. Paul Getty Museum Trust, which was put forth for the establishment of the center. Along with Vincent van Gogh's masterpiece Irises, the grounds beautiful garden is a must-see.

Smithsonian National Air and Space Museum in Washington, D.C.

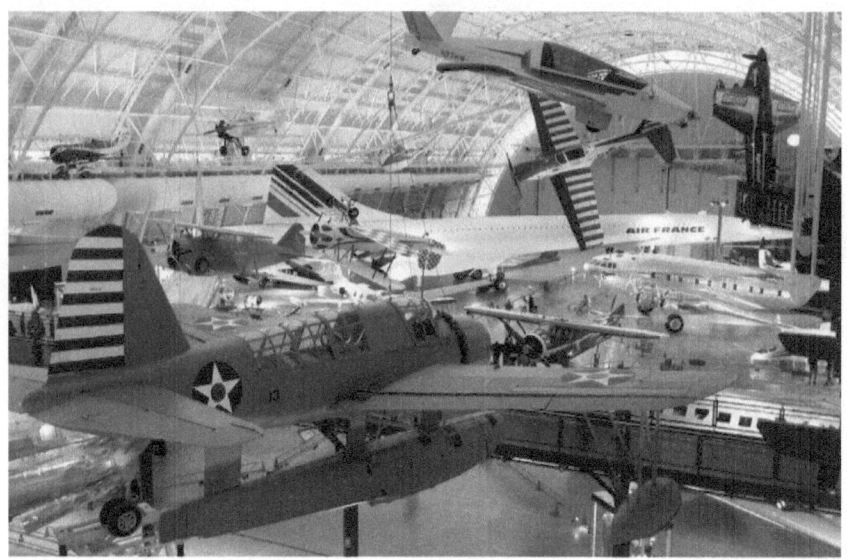

While the Smithsonian National Air and Space Museum didn't officially open until 1976, the institution's relation to aviation began at its creation with the first secretary of the Smithsonian, Joseph Henry. The physicist invited aeronaut Thaddeus S.C. Lowe to inflate a hot air balloon on the museum's grounds in 1861, establishing the institution's dedication to air and space education. The museum details America's storied past of space exploration and aeronautics trial and error.

Instituto Ricardo Brennand in Recife, Brazil

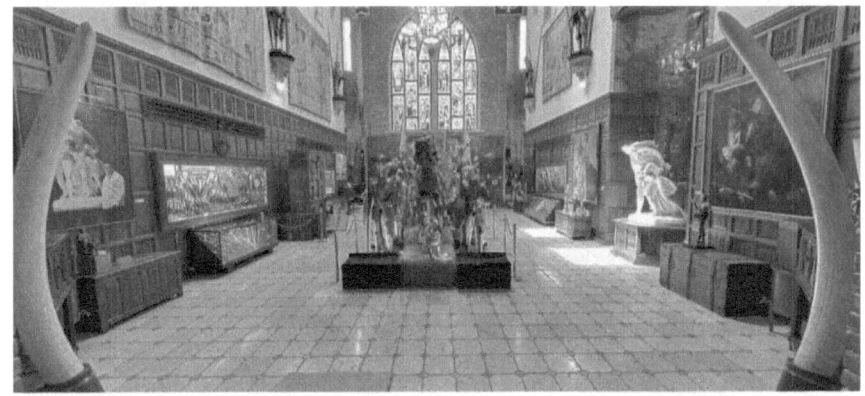

Brazilian collector and businessman Ricardo Brennand inaugurated the nonprofit cultural institution in 2002 with historic and artistic objects related to Colonial and Dutch Brazil. Instituto Ricardo Brennand's architecture is inspired by a Tudor-style castle complete with drawbridge. The colonial Brazil museum features an impressive collection of 3,000 pieces of armory.

Yad Vashem Holocaust Memorial in Jerusalem

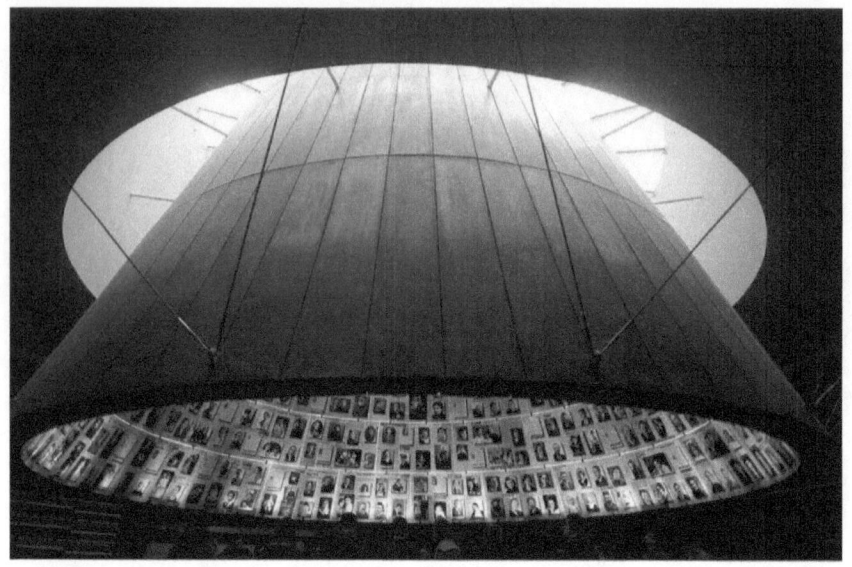

Yad Vashem serves as the World Holocaust Remembrance Center with its most notable installations being the Hall of Names, a memorial for each Jewish person murdered in the Holocaust. Designed by renowned architect Moshe Safdie, the center is located on Mount Herzi, also called the Mount of Remembrance, overlooking Jerusalem. The museum presents the story of the Holocaust through a Jewish perspective with original artifacts from victims, survivor testimonies, and personal possessions.

National Gallery of Art in Washington, D.C.

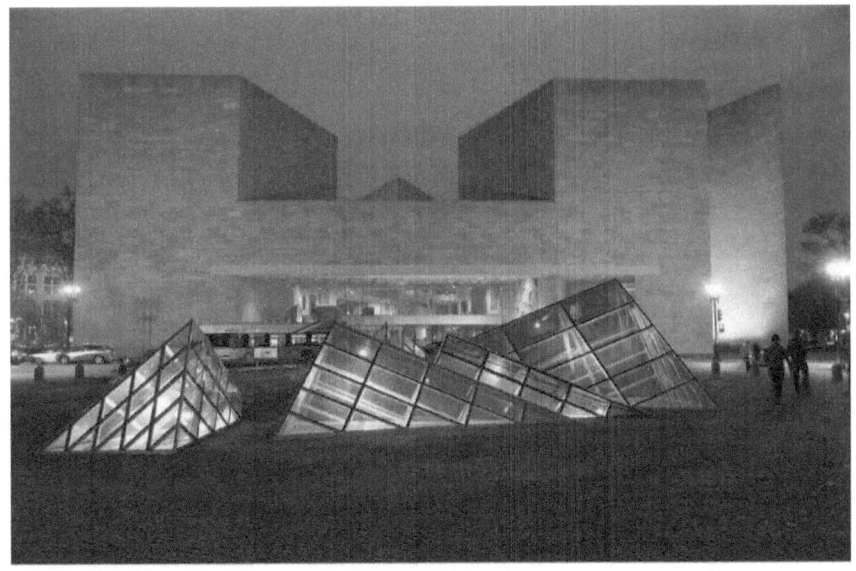

The 1937 creation of the National Gallery of Art is largely in part due to art collector and former secretary of the treasury, Andrew W. Mellon. The art enthusiast offered his expansive art collection to President Franklin D. Roosevelt for a new museum on the National Mall's grounds to equal the national art museums of other countries.

Architect John Russell Pope modeled the rotunda in the West Building after the ancient Roman Pantheon with barrel-vaulted sculpture halls to the east and west of it. The gallery provides a permanent home for nearly 4,000 European and American paintings, 3,000 sculptures, 31,000 drawings, 70,000 prints, and 12,000 photographs.

Inhotim in Brumadinho, Brazil

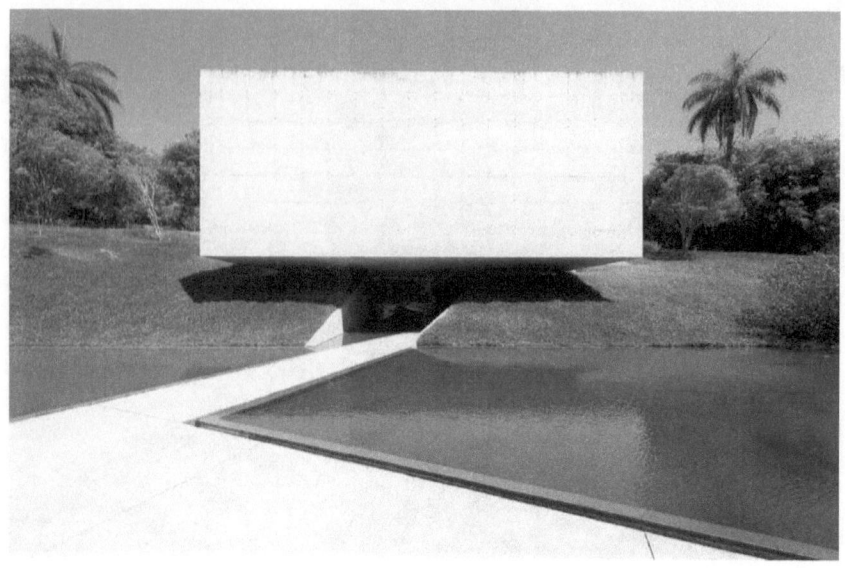

Inhotim houses one of the largest collections of contemporary art in Brazil along with one of the largest outdoor art centers in all of Latin America. As a way to protect the natural landscape surrounding his farmhouse in the mid-1980s, Minas Gerais businessman Bernardo de Mello Paz began buying the land surrounding the property. Soon after, Paz laid the foundation for Inhotim by converting his ranch into a 5,000-acre botanical garden. The gardens are now famous for containing rare species of plants from every continent.

Museo de Arte Latinoamericano de Buenos Aires

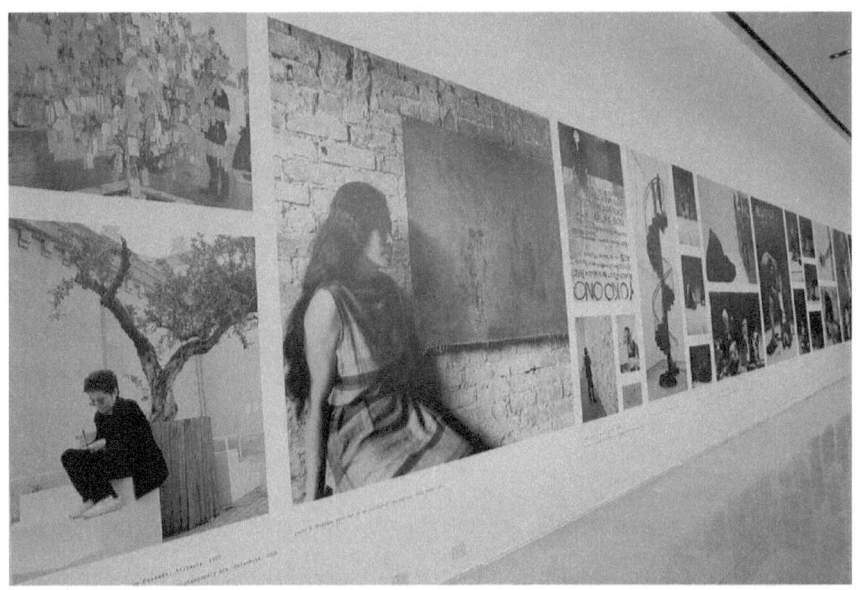

This Argentine museum showcases Latin American art spanning from the early 20th century to the present, including works from acclaimed artists like Frida Kahlo. The nonprofit museum was created by businessman Eduardo Costantini in 2001 with the museum's permanent body of work coming from his personal Costantini collection.

Museum of New Zealand Te Papa Tongarewa in Wellington

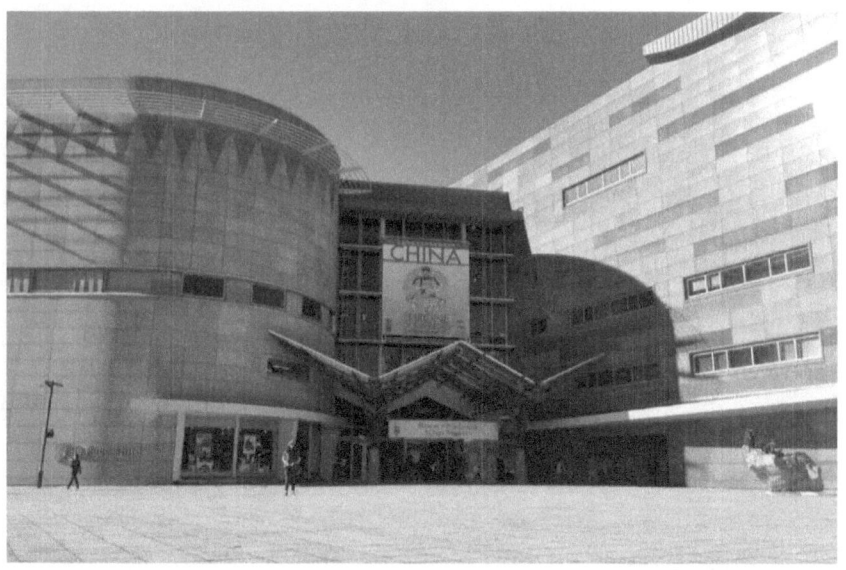

Explore the bicultural partnership between indigenous and nonindigenous people at New Zealand's national museum. Translated to "Our Place," Te Pa's emphasis on diversity began in 1865 with the opening of the Colonial Museum, which included a number of paintings and ethnographic items from the indigenous Māori people.

After a number of name changes, the Museum of New Zealand Te Papa Tongarewa officially opened 1998, uniting National Museum and National Art Gallery as one entity. The vast 800,000 piece collection ranges from contemporary artworks to ancestral carvings in their Taonga Māori Collection.

www.ingramcontent.com/pod-product-compliance
Lightning Source LLC
Chambersburg PA
CBHW030528220526
45463CB00007B/2756